M000197633

Witches

*"Any book without a mistake in it has had
too much money spent on it"*
Sir William Collins, publisher

Witches

NIGEL SUCKLING

Witches

Published by
Facts, Figures & Fun, an imprint of
AAPPL Artists' and Photographers' Press Ltd.
10 Hillside, London SW19 4NH, UK
info@ffnf.co.uk www.ffnf.co.uk
info@aappl.com www.aappl.com

Sales and Distribution
UK and export: Turnaround Publisher Services Ltd.
orders@turnaround-uk.com
USA and Canada: Sterling Publishing Inc.
sales@sterlingpub.com
Australia & New Zealand: Peribo Pty.
peribomec@bigpond.com
South Africa: Trinity Books. trinity@iafrica.com

A catalogue record for this book is available
from the British Library.

ISBN 13: 9781904332473
ISBN 10: 1904332471

Design (contents and cover): Malcolm Couch
mal.couch@blueyonder.co.uk

Printed in China by Imago Publishing
info@imago.co.uk

Contents

Introduction

In the caldron boil and bake;

Eye of newt, and toe of frog,
Wool of bat, and tongue of dog,
Adder's fork, and blind-worm's sting,
Lizard's leg, and owlet's wing, –
For a charm of powerful trouble,
Like a hell-broth boil and bubble.

ALL: *Double, double, toil and trouble;*
Fire burn and caldron bubble.

Macbeth Act IV Scene 1

In the theatre Shakespeare's *Macbeth* is a famously unlucky play despite its eternal popularity with audiences. Company members are supposed not to mention it by name anywhere within a theatre and must rather call it something oblique like 'the Scottish play' or 'the bard's play'.

According to Cassell's *Companion to Theatre* (1997) any actor saying 'Macbeth' in a theatre must leave the room, spin three times, spit or break wind, then knock on the door and ask permission to re-enter.

Some believers in the curse say it was conjured by Scottish witches dismayed by Shakespeare's portrayal of them. Others say that the playwright put real spells in his actors' mouths and these attract bad luck. Either way, Shakespeare did witches no favours, especially as witch-hunts were flaring up throughout Britain at the time, especially in Scotland. The last thing they needed was more encouragement for the general populace to see them as trouble-making crones who used babies in their brews ("Finger of birth-strangled babe / Ditch-deliver'd by a drab").

Rationalists believe the superstition arose simply because the play's popularity has always meant that cash-strapped theatrical companies tend to fall back on it as a last resort, just before the bailiffs arrive.

The play is believed to have been first performed in London in 1606 before the recently crowned King James I at Hampton Court. Richard Burbage played Macbeth and the boy actor Edmans his queen.

As King James VI of Scotland, the monarch had taken active part in the North Berwick witch trials of 1596. These led to the execution of about seventy alleged witches, many of them for trying to sink the king's ship by conjuring storms at sea.

The trials became famous across Europe through lurid news broadsides like those that popularised the infamous deeds of Dracula in eastern Europe, the werewolf Peter

Stubbe in Germany and the cannibal Sawney Beane in Scotland. The trials also prompted King James to publish his own book *Daemonologie* in 1597 which became a handbook for British witch finders.

It is unlikely Shakespeare himself visited Scotland at this time, but his actors Lawrence Fletcher & Company visited North Berwick in October 1601 when gossip about the trials still ran high. It seems likely that they provided Shakespeare with much colourful detail for his witch scenes.

The history behind *Macbeth* comes from Hector Boyce (or Boece)'s *History of Scotland* published in seventeen volumes in 1527 and translated from Latin into English by John Bellenden a few years later.

The scenes in which the goddess Hecate, the Witch Queen, joins the three witches (Act III Scene 5; Act IV Scene 1) are believed to have been added or embroidered by a later hand for dramatic effect.

Like vampires, witches can be considered on every level from the sublime to the ridiculous, with a detour through creepy horror along the way.

Also like vampires they can be great comedians without losing their capacity to invoke real fear and awe in different circumstances. In children's fiction there are countless comical or friendly witches as in the *Worst Witch*

stories by Jill Murphy or the *Meg and Mog* books by Helen Nicoll and Jan Pienkowski. But there remain scary ones, like the witches in *The Wizard of Oz* or *Narnia* tales which, despite their comfortable familiarity for adults, are still capable of provoking nightmares in impressionable young children.

As angels, holly, bells and mulled wine are to Christmas, so witches, vampires, werewolves and hobgoblins are to Halloween; but where witches differ from their Halloween companions is that they are not fundamentally wicked at all. Werewolves are naturally vicious and vampires just have to suck blood but witches have never automatically caused mischief. The pointy-hatted cackling crone riding a broomstick as she spreads havoc and mischief is largely a fiction of her enemies.

Of course there must have been witches through the ages that fit the stereotype quite closely, just as you find unpleasant people in any walk of life, but the wicked witch of popular superstition is as much a phantom as the vampire or werewolf. As with them, there is enough substance in the myth to make it horribly persuasive under the right conditions, but it's probably safe to say that most of the unfortunates who have met nasty ends through being accused of witchcraft were innocent of anything more than being unpopular with their neighbours.

Here in the twenty-first century West there is a large and still growing revival of interest in witchcraft in its positive

aspects, and on all levels from comedy and light entertainment to deep spiritual conviction. Children's and
young adult sections of bookshops are packed with titles
featuring good witches even before you arrive at the
Harry Potter or *Discworld* shelves.

There is also much interest in its dark side of course but,
as ever, the two do not necessarily go hand in hand. What
we are going to consider in this little book is anything of
interest about witchcraft, good or bad, that comes to
hand.

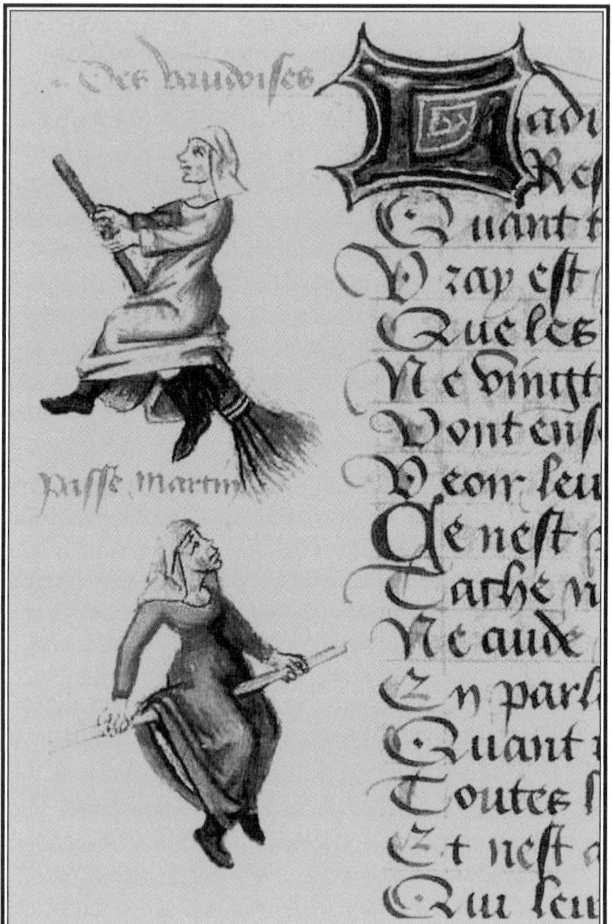
vaudises
Pisse martin

CHAPTER I

Hecate Unveiled: Myths and Legends

Hecate has been called the Queen of Witches from ancient times right through to the present.

Her origins in Greek mythology are slightly obscure but Hesiod's *Theogony* written about 700 BC says that when Zeus and the Olympian gods overthrew Cronos (Saturn) and his Titans to seize heaven, he permitted the Titan Hecate to keep all her powers. She was said to be the only deity apart from Zeus himself who could grant to or withhold from humans anything she wished.

Some say that Hecate was a midwife at Zeus's birth and helped save him from being eaten by his father Cronos, a favour Zeus later repaid.

Hesiod also says that Hecate was the daughter of Gaia (Earth) and Uranus (Sky). She was given power over the sky, earth and underworld and is often shown as triple-formed to reflect this, sometimes being named Hecate

Selene (Moon), Hecate Artemis (Diana the Huntress) and Hecate Persephone.

There are other accounts of her parentage though. All that is clear is that she enjoyed wide reverence in the ancient Greek world and had a chapel in the famous Temple of Artemis (Diana) in Ephesus, one of the Seven Wonders of the ancient world.

Being able to pass freely between the three worlds is what gives Hecate her supreme command of magic. She sometimes wanders the earth at night to see how it fares, invisible to humans but dogs see her and that is when they bark and howl for no apparent reason.

Sometimes she is shown as maid, mother and crone, representing the three ages of woman.

As a personification of the Great Mother, Hecate was originally most associated with childbirth and raising children. Later the name became most linked with her crone aspect.

Hecate is the goddess of crossroads, especially those where three ways meet. When the ancient Greek dead arrived in Hades after crossing the River Styx she would greet them at the crossroads and help them choose the path they deserve: the Elysian Fields for the noble and heroic; the Fields of Asphodel for those who have led blameless but timid lives; or Tartarus, a joyless and dim land for sinners.

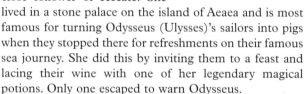

Circe was an enchantress and close follower of Hecate. She lived in a stone palace on the island of Aeaea and is most famous for turning Odysseus (Ulysses)'s sailors into pigs when they stopped there for refreshments on their famous sea journey. She did this by inviting them to a feast and lacing their wine with one of her legendary magical potions. Only one escaped to warn Odysseus.

When Odysseus went to rescue his men, a youth fell in with him on the path through the woods that surrounded Circe's palace. It was the god Hermes (Mercury) in human guise who gave him a sprig of the herb *moly*, which has a black root and a white flower. Hermes warned Odysseus of the danger awaiting him but said the herb would protect him from Circe's drugged wine.

Circe welcomed Odysseus and feasted him as she had the others. But when at the end of the meal she tapped him with a wand and told him to join his friends in the pigsty, all that happened was that he drew his sword and held it

MEDEA

MEDEA, another famous witch from Greek mythology, was Circe's niece, the daughter of her brother King Aetes of Colchis, now a territory of modern Georgia. When Jason came that way in quest of the Golden Fleece she fell in love and helped him by magical means to overcome the otherwise impossible tasks he faced.

King Aetes had told Jason he could have the Fleece if, like Hercules, he first performed a few labours. First he had to plough a field with fire-breathing oxen with bronze hooves that he had to yoke himself. Then he had to sow the field with dragons' teeth that would immediately spring up as armed warriors to attack him. Then he would have to kill the sleepless dragon that guarded the Fleece itself.

Well, Medea gave Jason a spell to calm the oxen so he could yoke them. She also gave him a charmed stone that he threw among the warriors when they attacked, so that they turned on each other. And she gave him a sleeping potion to sprinkle over the dragon so that he could slip the Fleece away from under it and sail away with Medea as his bride.

Later, when Jason was bemoaning the age and infirmity of his father, Medea offered to make him young again. Under a full moon she called upon Hecate and a chariot drawn by flying serpents came to carry her away to distant lands to gather the rare herbs and other ingredients for the spell.

Nine nights she was engaged in this labour, during which time she spoke to no other person.

Next she sacrificed a black sheep to Hebe, Hecate's incarnation as the goddess of youth, and collected its blood in a cauldron. Then she made Jason's father fall into a deep sleep and mixed into the cauldron all the ingredients she had gathered – the herbs and precious stones, hoar-frost gathered by moonlight, a screech-owl's head and wings, the entrails of a wolf, the head and beak of a crow and countless other ingredients, stirring them in with a dry olive branch.

Suddenly the branch burst into leaf and, seizing the moment, Medea cut the old man's throat so all his blood gushed out. Then into the wound and his mouth she poured the contents of her cauldron. In no time his wrinkles eased and colour returned to his head and beard; new blood coursed in his veins and he sat up feeling forty years younger.

Medea was also able to turn her talents to darker purposes, however. When Jason abandoned her to marry the princess of Corinth, she sent the bride a poisoned gown that killed her. Then, killing all her own children by Jason and setting fire to her palace, Medea mounted her serpent-drawn chariot and flew off to Athens where she married King Aegeus.

at her throat till she promised to undo the enchantment. More than that, she fell in love with him and entertained him so well that for a while he forgot all about his journey.

Finally after a year Odysseus came to his senses and although Circe was reluctant to see him go, she armed him with knowledge of the dangers ahead, including the Sirens and the twin perils of Scylla and Charybdis – the many-headed monster and the whirlpool.

Circe was responsible for the monstrous Scylla in the first place. She had once been a fair maiden who had stolen the heart of Circe's lover Glaucus and paid for it by being turned into a snaky monster.

One of the most famous witches of non-classical legend is Morgan le Fay, King Arthur's half-sister and nemesis. She first appears in the twelfth century *Life of Merlin* by Geoffrey of Monmouth where she is represented as a healer and shapeshifter, possibly one of the faery folk of ancient Britain. She also ruled over the Isle of Avalon with her sisters.

In the early tales Morgan le Fay is a benevolent figure but in Malory's *Morte d'Arthur* she is portrayed mainly as a malevolent witch constantly plotting Arthur's downfall. In some versions of the legend she tricks Arthur by magic into sleeping with her and thus conceiving Mordred, who eventually kills Arthur and usurps his throne. But slightly paradoxically she is also supposed to be one of the queens who come to carry his body away by boat to Avalon (the Island of Apples) after his mortal wound at the Battle of Cammlan.

> *The Island of Apples, which is called the Fortunate Isle has its name because it produces all things for itself. There is no work for the farmers in ploughing the fields, all cultivation is absent except for what nature manages by herself. On its own the island produces fertile crops and grapes and native apples by means of its own trees in the cropped pastures. On its own the overflowing soil puts forth all things in addition to the grass, and in that place one lives for a hundred years or more. There nine sisters give pleasant laws to those who come from our parts to them, and of those sisters, she who is higher becomes a doctor in the art of healing and exceeds her sisters in excellent form. Morgen is her name, and she has learned what usefulness all the herbs bear so that she may cure sick bodies. Also that art is known to her by which she can change shape and cut the air on new wings in the manner of Daedalus.*

Geoffrey of Monmouth *Vita Merlini* (c.1150)

THE WITCH OF BERKELEY

William of Malmesbury recorded the remarkable tale of the Witch of Berkeley which he had heard from someone who claimed to have witnessed the events at first hand in 1065.

He heard that in Berkeley, Gloucestershire, there once lived an old witch whose familiar was a jackdaw (or a chough according to Reinulph of Chester's version).

She had three children – one married, one a monk and one a nun. She happily practised her witchcraft for many years but one day her jackdaw informed her that her married son had been killed in an accident and all his family now faced ruin.

She took this as a sign that God had finally lost patience with her and was going to exact vengeance for all her wicked ways despite the prayers of her pious children (the story is being told to us by a monk!). So she sent for her surviving offspring, the monk and the nun, and told them that there might be no way of saving her soul from hell, but if they followed her instructions they might save her body from it.

When she died they were to sew her up in a stag's hide and lay her in a stone coffin "fast bound and cemented with iron and lead". They were to stand this on end and bind it further with three iron chains. Then they were to pay in advance to have Mass said each morning for forty days, and psalms to be sung each night. If after doing all this, her body lay at rest for three days and nights then on the fourth it would be safe to bury it in the churchyard.

Well, when she died they followed her instructions precisely, but to no avail. On the very first night some demons broke down the church doors and managed to snap one of the iron chains. On the second night they came and broke a second. Then on the third night towards cock-crow there came the mightiest demon so far, Satan himself some believed, who broke the third iron chain, smashed the stone coffin open and commanded the dead witch to rise. She did, and then was dragged outside and set upon a ghostly black horse neighing by the door. It thundered away with her and the screaming was heard for four miles. And that was the last of the old Witch of Berkeley.

QUEEN OF THE WITCHES

DURING THE INFAMOUS witch trials in Scotland in the sixteenth and seventeenth centuries, most confessions were extracted by torture. A notable exception is that of Isobel Gowdie, a young housewife from Auldearne near Nairn, who is sometimes called Queen of the Witches because without apparent coercion she gave one of the most vivid portraits of what everyone believed about witches at the time.

Gowdie admitted to having sexual intercourse with the Devil, commenting on the extreme cold of his penis. She also was a frequent visitor to faeryland or Elphame. Where she had been entertained at feasts by the magnificent Queen Elf herself in one of her palaces under the hills. Unlike most humans who taste faery food she had been able to come and go from Elphame as she pleased. The entrance to faeryland, she said, was guarded by elf-bulls whose roaring always scared her.

The faeries, said Isobel, had taught her to fly by mounting beanstalks or cornbails and shouting "Horse and Hattock in the Devil's Name!" Along with other witches and faeries, Gowdie would change into animal form, most often a hare or cat, to work mischief among their neighbours for entertainment.

When she went to a witches' sabbat, Isobel claimed she would slip her broomstick into her place in bed and her husband never noticed or guessed what she was about.

She also claimed to be able to turn herself into a cat. To do so, she would repeat the following three times:

> *I shall goe intill ane catt,*
> *With sorrow, and sych, and a blak shott;*
> *And I shall goe in the Divellis name,*
> *Ay will I com home againe.*

To change back into her human form, she would say the following three times:

> *Catt, catt, God send thee a blak shott.*
> *I am in a cattis likness just now,*
> *But I shall be in a womanis likness even now.*
> *Catt, catt, God send thee a blak shott*

Opinion is divided over whether Isobel Gowdie was executed for witchcraft but there is no reason to believe she escaped being strangled and burned, the standard punishment for witchcraft at the time. Memory of her remarkable claims has lived on to the present day in ballads and even novels; while *The Confessions of Isobel Gowdie* is a symphonic piece by the Scottish composer James MacMillan that premiered to great acclaim at the London Proms in 1990, performed by the Scottish Symphony Orchestra. Macmillan said that it was "The Requiem that Isobel Gowdie never had" and that it "offers Isobel Gowdie the mercy and humanity that was denied her in the last days of her life".

CHAPTER II

The Craft:
Tools and Practices

There's an old woman dwells upon Tappington Moor,
She hath years on her back at the least fourscore,
And some people fancy a great many more;
Her nose it is hook'd,
Her back it is crook'd,
Her eyes blear and red:
On the top of her head
Is a shocking bad hat,
Extinguisher-shaped, the brim narrow and flat!
Then, - My Gracious! - her beard! - it would
   sadly perplex
A spectator at first to distinguish her sex;
Nor, I'll venture to say, without scrutiny could be

Pronounce her, off-handed, a Punch or Judy.
Did you see her, in short, that mud-hovel within,
With her knees to her nose, and her nose to her chin,
Leering up with that queer, indescribable grin,
You'd lift up your hands in amazement, and cry,
'- Well! - I never did see such a regular Guy!'

Thomas Ingoldsby *The Hand of Glory* (1840)

But seriously, it's doubtful that witches ever looked much like their fairytale stereotype – except to the degree that during the great witch hunts the majority of victims were old, poor women who lived alone. In most old engravings witches are shown wearing whatever headgear was prevailing at the time.

What has come to be seen as the traditional witch's pointy hat possibly derives from the normal headgear popular with Puritans in the seventeenth century, and persisting much longer in places like Wales where it is considered traditional costume. More likely is that it comes from the conical black hat that the Spanish Inquisition used to put on the heads of heretics before they were burned.

These days you could pass a witch in the street without knowing it from their dress, though often there is some giveaway detail like a discreet pentacle or silver moon among their jewellery. There's also a high probability that if you come across a group of people dancing naked in the woods around a bonfire, they will be witches. But except on ceremonial occasions most modern witches dress like everybody else.

Traditional Ways to Guard Against Witches

In Scotland witches can be kept away by hiding or burying old shoes in the north east corner of a house, the point at which it is most vulnerable to supernatural entry. In most countries, though, the front threshold and chimney are considered the most vulnerable spots. Scattering seeds on the threshold, throwing salt on the fire or hanging garlic, rue and indeed old boots around the doors and windows will all guard against hostile witchcraft. These precautions should especially be taken if your candles burn with a blue flame, because that is a sign that someone is seeking to harm you by magical means.

Witch bottles (see overleaf)

A useful charm against witchcraft is to bind twigs of rowan, ash and birch together with a red thread and carry them on your person. Their combined virtues will turn away any malicious spell.

Rue, groundsel, radish and garlic also turn away evil intent when worn or carried.

If a person seems to be under enchantment, one way to find out who is casting the spell is to bake a Witch Cake. Take the normal ingredients of a cake and add to them the urine of the afflicted person. Bake the cake and feed it to a dog. The dog should then lead you to the sorcerer.

Collect 'witch stones', stones and pebbles with a natural hole and hang then around the areas you want to protect or wear them as jewellery.

WITCH BOTTLES

An ancient and well-tried means of deflecting malicious spells (or indeed any bad intent) is the witch bottle. They are now largely forgotten but for hundreds of years across Europe and other continents they were considered a mainstay of rural families against the forces of darkness.

Witch bottles still often turn up during the demolition or restoration of old buildings and over 200 exist in known collections. These are probably just a tiny fraction of those found over the years and simply smashed or thrown away.

The most popular hiding places for them were under the hearthstone or doorstep of a house, its most vulnerable points for intrusion. But they were also often plastered into walls or chimneys, hidden in attics or buried in out of the way places away from the house.

The idea of a witch bottle was to create a magical decoy that would trick hostile enchantments into thinking they had found the maker, and then trap them. The principle is almost the same as with voodoo dolls, but with reverse intent. So hair, nail clippings and bodily fluids went into the bottle. People usually urinated into it but some added blood for added potency. Often people drew a face or wrote their name on wood or paper and added that to the mix.

Then, having created the simulacrum or decoy, people added snares to catch the spell – thorns, bent nails and fish-hooks, anything sharp and snagging. Other common ingredients were tangled balls of thread or wool to confuse the enchantment, and

sometimes deadly nightshade and other poisonous herbs. Then, no doubt with some ritual and chanting, the bottle was buried, probably under a new moon.

From the sixteenth to the eighteenth centuries Bellarmine jars were very popular for witch bottles across Europe. These were named after the unpopular sixteenth century Cardinal whose bearded face was first stamped on them in the Netherlands, but copies were made in other countries. They were stoneware jugs with handles commonly used in taverns for taking wine from cask to table. From a magical point of view their attraction was having a face on the bottle which made the simulacrum even more convincing. These bottles were also popular for burying money, no doubt with spells cast on them to deflect treasure hunters.

BROOMSTICKS

Flying broomsticks are an essential part of the Halloween witch's equipment but the idea only really caught on in the sixteenth and seventeenth centuries. Before that, witches were equally known for flying on the backs of goats, cats, owls and many other creatures.

In pagan fertility rites participants would ride shovels, forks and brooms like hobby-horses around the bonfires.

Original brooms were made from the broom plant or birch twigs tied together.

In medieval times the broom or besom was a symbol of domesticity, of the woman's realm. Because most witches

were female the broom became their symbol by
association.

An element of the witch hysteria was probably men's fear
of women being too powerful. A witch defying nature by
riding her broom through the night sky is a perfect
symbol of this. There are accounts of male witches riding
broomsticks but more commonly they chose pitchforks.

Some witches are believed to have used their brooms in a
quite literal manner for 'flying', smearing the handle with
hallucinogenic salve and then 'riding' it to ingest the
drugs through the sensitive skin of their private parts.
This probably also accounted for rumours of orgiastic
goings-on at witches' sabbats, though it's now impossible
to judge how common the practice has ever been.

Ingesting these often deadly potions through the skin
reduces the risk of overdosing on them. Broomsticks were
probably popular because the wooden handle would have
been worn smooth through use.

Ingredients known to have been used in flying potions or
salves include deadly nightshade (belladonna), henbane
(*Hyoscyamus Niger*), hemlock (*Conium Maculatum*) and
aconite root (*Aconitum Napellus*).

Another common hallucinogen that was often taken acci-
dentally was ergot, a mould that commonly forms in rye
bread. As towns grew in the sixteenth and seventeenth

centuries, bread tended to be less fresh than in country villages, giving the mould more chance to develop. Many outbreaks of madness from the late Middle Ages onward have been blamed on ergot poisoning and this led to the growing popularity of wheat bread, which is resistant to ergot mould. Many witches however deliberately cultivated ergot for their flying salves.

Norfolk, Suffolk and neighbouring counties in East Anglia are notable not only for their apparent abundance of witches but for the continued popularity of rye bread there after it had fallen from favour elsewhere.

Usually witches are supposed to ride their broomsticks with the handle pointing forward but in the seventeenth century there were tales of witches flying them the other way, with lanterns or flares in the bristles to light the way.

Besides their usefulness for flying, broomsticks could also be charmed to resemble a person, usually the witch herself to disguise her absence when out gallivanting.

In modern witchcraft brooms are often used to cleanse an area spiritually before rituals commence.

When, for one reason or another, witches did not want to fly to a gathering in the old days, they could always bewitch someone to carry them there, it seems. In 1673 Anne Armstrong living near Stocksfield on Tyne claimed she had been enchanted to carry several local witches to a gathering. She said that a witch called Anne Forster had put a bridle on her that changed her into the likeness of a horse. Then she had "rid upon her cross-legged till they came to the rest of her companions at Riding mill bridge end, where they usually met". There the bridle was removed and she resumed her normal shape.

CAULDRONS

Ever since Circe and Medea the cauldron has been another essential item of witch paraphernalia. This is where the witch brews her love potions and remedies, or curses and poisons depending on the circumstances.

Witches often carry their cauldrons with them when flying to gatherings because they like to perform their magic in the open air.

Certain witches' brews when tipped into the sea from a cauldron could raise storms, but this was not always necessary. Witches were once supposed to have a multitude of ways to raise storms and for many hundred years most freak weather events were blamed on them. Good witches however were believed equally able to conjure good weather.

Symbolically the cauldron represents the womb of the Great Goddess and is related to the Holy Grail, the Chalice, the cornucopia, alchemists' crucibles and the Celtic Cauldrons of Plenty.

Filled with water, the witch's cauldron can also be used to see future or distant events, but most witches are equally able to see them in wells, crystals or magic mirrors.

MAGIC MIRRORS

Albertus Magnus, the famous medieval scholar
and alchemist, records that a magic mirror or
speculum for seeing distant or future events could
be made the following way:

1. Buy a mirror and incribe upon it "S. Solam,
S. Tattler, S. Echogordner Gematur"

2. Bury it at a crossroads at an odd hour

3. After three days return to the crossroads at
the same hour and retrieve it

4. Do not be the first person to look into the
mirror. Let a stray dog or cat look into it first
[so they catch the bad luck] and then see what
the mirror has to tell you

To see the face of your future partner, walk backwards
out of the house on a bright moonlit night while gazing
on a hand mirror and repeating the following:

> *Around and around, O stars so fair!*
> *You travel and search out everywhere;*
> *I pray you, sweet stars, now show to me*
> *The face of my lover who is to be.*

A mirror can also be used to snare a lover
using the following directions:

1. Find a hand mirror with a backing of
   copper, Venus's metal

2. Inscribe the name of the desired one
   and the symbol of their birth sign on the
   back of the mirror

3. Take the mirror to where a dog and
   bitch are mating and watch them
   in the mirror

4. Lend the mirror to the subject of the
   spell and they will immediately be
   overcome with lust for you

THE HAND OF GLORY

In black magic much use is made of
human body parts, each having its own
virtue. One of the most potent magical
tools is the Hand of Glory candlestick.
These have become rare since criminals
ceased to be left rotting on the gibbet at
empty crossroads, but mummified ones
still turn up occasionally and are to be
found in museums. The one in Whitby

Museum is one of their most popular exhibits, especially with children.

The Hand of Glory was mainly used by burglars because for as long as it was lit in a house no householder would wake, as memorably described in *The Ingoldsby Legends* (1840).

> *Wherever that terrible light shall burn,*
> *Vainly the sleeper may toss and turn;*
> *His leaden eyes shall he ne'er unclose*
> *So long as that magical taper glows,*
> *Life and treasure shall he command*
> *Who knoweth the charm of the Glorious Hand.*

The prescription for making a Hand was this:

◆ Go to a crossroads gallows at midnight and cut off either hand of the criminal corpse there, and pull some hair from its head.

◆ Wrap the hand in a strip of shroud and squeeze any remaining blood out of it.

◆ Put the hand in an earthenware pot and soak in a mash of saltpetre, zimort (cinnamon), common salt and peppercorns for two weeks.

◆ Expose to bright sunlight, preferably during the time of the dog-star (July 3-August 11) till all fat has drained from the hand. Alternatively, bake gently in an oven with vervain and bracken.

◆ Collect the fat and mix with horse dung, Lapland sesame and virgin wax and make your candle with the hair for a wick.

◆ Set your candle between the hand's fingers and you are ready. Light it in a house and everyone who is asleep there will be unable to wake until it is extinguished.

Unless, that is, the householder has taken preventative measures. To guard against the use of a Hand of Glory one should make a paste from the fat of a white hen, the blood of a screech owl and the gall of a black cat. If this is smeared on thresholds, window frames and chimneys a Hand of Glory will not work.

WITCHES AND SATAN

In Britain and much of the rest of Europe in the bad old days it was believed that the first step in becoming a witch was to make a compact with Satan, though he is rarely called that. Generally he is described as a 'dark lord', a 'black-robed man' or by more colourful names such as 'the lord of the forest'; or by Biblical sounding names such as Antecessoar in one case in Sweden, or Mamilion in England.

It is unlikely that many witches at the time saw this figure as Satan (if they made a compact with any spirit at all) but he might well have been one of the old horned woodland gods such as Cernunnos or Herne the Hunter, who would naturally have been seen as the Devil by Church inquisitors.

If not Satan himself, this figure was seen by witches' enemies as one of his demons, or one of their servants in

a chain of hierarchy connecting with the Devil. In the Salem witch trials of Massachusetts he was identified by the accusing girls as a former minister of the congregation.

After the compact is sealed (often by a kiss to the Devil's backside according to the wildest imaginings, but more commonly by signing his book) it was believed that the witch was given one or more 'familiars', minor demons which would thenceforth act as a go-between, communicating Satan's wishes to the witch, and the witch's desires to Satan. This could be any kind of animal or even an undisguised demon, but was most commonly a cat, hare or toad that would suck the witch's blood from a secret extra nipple as payment for its services.

THE WITCH'S CAT

Cats have been associated with witchcraft (in both its positive and negative aspects) since at least the time of ancient Egypt where the cat goddess Bast was said to be the daughter of Isis and Osiris.

Common cats in Egypt were believed to be the eyes of Horus, Bast's brother, by means of which he followed what was going on in the world. Killing a cat was considered a sacrilege punishable by death and many were mummified with as much care as was given to important humans.

According to Diodorus Siculus a Roman soldier was lynched in Egypt in the first century BC for killing a cat, despite pleas to the mob by King Ptolemy, who feared Roman retribution.

There is no mention of cats in the Bible, something that witch-hunting Puritans saw as a mark of God's mistrust of them.

I know from mine own experience that certain women when prowling about at night in the form of cats have been espied by those who were quietly watching in silence and in secret. When these animals have been wounded, upon the very next day the women bear on their bodies in the numerical place the wounds inflicted on the cat, and if so a limb has been chopped off the animal, they have lost a corresponding member.

Gervase of Tilbury *Otia Imperialia* twelfth century

In Scotland a famous gathering of cats at the fish market in Aberdeen on Halloween 1595 was believed to be a convention of witches.

At an enquiry in Caithness in 1718 a mason, William Montgomery, testified that his nights had been disturbed by the howling of cats, which he believed to be witches. One night he had lost patience and attacked them with a sword and hatchet, killing two and wounding another. The next day two local women were found dead and a third, Margaret Nin-Gilbert, had so deep a hatchet wound in one leg that it eventually withered and dropped off.

Dorothy Ellis, a Cambridgeshire witch, confessed in 1647 that the Devil had appeared to her in the likeness of a great cat that made promises to her and then demanded blood, which she gave and thereafter would let him suck blood as he wished. With the aid of this cat she claimed to have killed one neighbour's cattle and lamed another. With a third she crippled his wife and caused fits in their infant until it died.

In her *Traditions of Devonshire* 1838 Mrs Bray tells of a Tavistock woman famous for being able to turn into a hare. Her grandson profited by tipping off hunters where

they might spot a hare. He then took his finder's fee but
the hare always got away. Till finally after a close and long
hunt the hare was chased into the woman's cottage where
the hunters found only her, scratched and bleeding and
panting deeply as though after a long chase . . .

In Britain cats and hares were the most common forms
that witches were supposed to adopt for travelling abroad
at night, but they could also take the form of dogs. In
mainland Europe where wolves survived much longer in
the wild any unusually aggressive wolf behaviour was also
attributed to witchcraft and there was a broad overlap
between witchcraft and lycanthropy.

In Samlesbury, Lancashire, in 1612, fourteen-year-old
Grace Sowerbutts accused her grandmother, aunt and
their friend Jane Southworth of being witches. Among
other charges was that they sometimes roamed the country as black dogs. To transform they used a magic oint-
ment derived from the body parts of a child they had
kidnapped and murdered. Grace also accused them of
having cooked some of the child's flesh and inviting her to
share their feast. All the accusations were proved to be
complete fabrications and the charges against the three
women dropped.

In Devonshire witches were often said to range the moor
in the form of black dogs. Folklorist Sabine Baring-Gould
in the mid nineteenth century heard the tale there of two
black dogs who took to visiting an inn and demanding
cider. When the landlord shot a silver bullet over their
heads they immediately transformed into two old women,
local witches.

WALPURGIS NIGHT

*I*N CONTINENTAL EUROPE there was, during the witch hunting years, much greater belief in witches' sabbats (great periodic gatherings of witches) than in Britain. In England particularly people usually saw witches as solitary or at most drawn to small groups of fellow spirits, relatively speaking anyway. Covens of thirteen were quite common and there are occasional mentions of larger groups, but there is no British equivalent to the tumultuous mass gatherings of witches and demons supposed to happen annually in Germany on Walpurgis Night.

Walpurgis Night on 30 April (May Eve) is when witches gather and celebrate on the Brocken, or Blocksberg, the myth and often mist-shrouded peak in the Harz Mountains that features in Goethe's *Faust* (1808):

> *Now to the Brocken the witches ride;*
> *The stubble is gold and the corn is green;*
> *There is the carnival crew to be seen,*
> *And Squire Urianus will come to preside.*
> *So over the valleys our company floats,*
> *With witches a-farting on stinking old goats.*

One reason for the Brocken's eerie reputation is the Spectre that occasionally looms out of the mist when the sun is low and scares the wits out of climbers to this day – a towering, shadowy figure often with a rainbow halo. Two of the mountain's rocks are known as the Devil's Pulpit and the Witches' Altar.

Walpurgis Night is named after St Walpurga, who was born in England in 710 but moved to Germany where she founded a number of convents before settling in Wurttenberg, where she was abbess of the convent of Heidenheim. After her death and burial at Eichstatt, healing oil was said to trickle from her tomb.

Walpurga was sainted on 1 May 779 and so was adopted for a Christianised version of the ancient pagan May Day festival for the first day of summer. This is at the opposite pole of the year to Halloween and is similarly a time when the gates between the visible and invisible worlds are flung open.

On Walpurgis Night farmers traditionally took precautions to save their cattle and other livestock from the witches who would be abroad, locking them in barns and sealing the doors with three crosses. Windows, chimneys and other possible points of entry were shielded with branches of ash, hawthorn, juniper and elder.

They were not just guarding against supernatural dangers. Walpurgis Night and St John's Eve were both nights when normally sane people were licensed to go a bit mad. As Hermann Sudermann expressed it in his 1905 play *St John's Fire* (Porter translation):

> For you see, pastor, within every one of us a spark of paganism is glowing. It has out-lasted the thousand years since the old Teutonic times. Once a year it flames up high, and we call it St. John's

Fire. Once a year comes Free-night. Yes, truly, Free-night. Then the witches, laughing scornfully, ride to Blocksberg, upon the mountain-top, on their broomsticks, the same broomsticks with which at other times their witchcraft is whipped out of them, then the whole wild company skims along the forest way, and then the wild desires awaken in our hearts which life has not fulfilled.

In Sweden where Walpurgis Night is known as *Valborg* and Finland where it is called *Vappu* this is one of the chief festivals of the year alongside Christmas and most people have the day off work to celebrate the arrival of summer with traditional songs and dance.

WALPURGIS NIGHT TRADITIONS

Horseshoes hung points upwards over a door
will keep witches and harm away this night.

If you wish to see a witch this night, wear
your clothes inside out and creep backwards
to a crossroads.

Gunshots fired over cornfields will keep
away blight.

If you hide in a cornfield you will see or hear
something that tells you how the next year will go.

If it rains on Walpurgis Night the crops will flourish,
but if it rains the next day they will be poor.

A heavy dew on May Morning signals a good
'butter year', and:

The fair maid who on the first of May
Goes to the fields at break of day
And washes in dew from the hawthorn tree
Will ever after beautiful be

If girls hear a cuckoo on May Day they can learn
how long it will be till their marriage by singing:

Cuckoo! cuckoo! on the bough
Tell me truly, tell me how
Many years there will be
Till a husband comes to me

WITCH FESTIVALS

All witches closely follow the cycles of the moon in parallel with those of the sun, celebrating the new, full and waning moon in different ways each month.

Then in the Wheel of the witches' year are eight major solar festivals, spaced roughly six weeks apart and based on the solstices and equinoxes. These are observed with equal enthusiasm by both White and Black witches. They were all once pagan agricultural festivals that to a greater or lesser extent were absorbed into the Christian Calendar.

◆ The witch New Year falls on Halloween, as it did for the ancient Celts and others. Other common names for this festival are Samhain, All Hallows Eve and Martinmas. It is the season when the gates between the visible and invisible worlds are briefly opened and for a while it is easy to cross from one side to the other. All kinds of spirits walk abroad on this night, not just ghosts, hobgoblins, banshees and the like but faeries, gnomes leprechauns and many other good sprites, though they are more mischievous than usual. All kinds of fortune telling work particularly well on Halloween.

◆ About six weeks later comes the winter solstice, better known as Christmas or Yule. Although Christmas comes a few days after the actual solstice, or shortest day, it is a continuation of the old pagan festival of excess called Saturnalia that evolved to distract agricultural people from the rigours of the winter ahead in northern climes.

◆ Next around 1 February comes Candlemas (Brigid's Night, Imbolc, Oimelc, Groundhog Day). Few non-witches pay much attention to this now but it was once a major festival celebrated with candles to represent the invisible stirring of plant life beneath the frozen earth. Its Celtic name *Imbolc* means 'in the womb', meaning the womb of Mother Earth; while *Oimelc* means 'ewe's milk' because this is the traditional lambing time. This is supposed to be the best night of the year for consulting oracles about one's love life. For witches it marks the first day of spring.

◆　Most of the pagan traditions of the Spring Equinox around 21 March (Lady Day) have been absorbed into the Christian festival of Easter, a movable feast determined by the phase of the moon in relation to the equinox. The Easter Bunny has evolved from the witches' hare, which traditionally goes mad at this time of year with lust and joy, while Easter Eggs reflect the returning fertility of the world. This feast marks the point at which in the old days people could afford to stop worrying so much about rationing their stores and start to anticipate the bounty of approaching summer.

◆　May Eve (it is notable that all witch festivals begin with nightfall), also known as Beltane or Walpurgis Night, sits opposite Halloween on the Wheel of the Year. Just as Halloween ushers in the dark and cold half of the year, so May Eve opens the bright half. Once again the boundaries between the visible and invisible worlds open and it becomes possible to cross either way. It is less threatening than Halloween though because the general mood of the world is uplifted and moving out of the shadows. In the old days May Eve and the following day were celebrated with maypoles and bonfires and dancing, and there was much wandering in the woods and on the hills. It was an occasion for romance and trysts between lovers, with a blind eye being turned to the usual proprieties in honour of the wedding feast of summer and winter.

◆ The Midsummer Solstice on 21 June is when people in England traditionally say, "Gosh it's Midsummer Day and we've had hardly any summer at all yet!" forgetting that the warmest weeks of the year have followed its longest day for even longer than they've been saying it, except in particularly strange years.

◆ Like Candlemas, its opposite on the Wheel of the Year, the eve of the 1 August (Lammas, Lughnasad, Feast of First Fruits) now receives little attention from non-witches, for whom it marks the first day of autumn, even though in the northern hemisphere the summer feels at its height. Its once popular name Lammas means loaf-mass because it celebrated the first bread baked from that year's harvest. It was the day for making corn dollies to bring luck for the main harvest which still lay ahead.

◆ The Autumn Equinox around 21 September (St Michael's Day, Harvest Home, John Barleycorn's Day) is traditionally the time for celebrating that the harvest is in and no longer at the mercy of the elements. The best and worst of the year's weather has happened and the result is known. Now all that remains is to pack nature's bounty safely into storage and start to batten down for the winter. On a non-agricultural level it was also the occasion for tying up loose ends and settling affairs so that everyone could settle into the more contemplative mood of winter without too many distractions.

◆ About six weeks later comes Halloween and the cycle begins again.

CHAPTER III

The Burning Times: Witches in History

At the end of the seventh century Theodore, Archbishop of Canterbury in England, drew up a code of penalties for witchcraft in his *Liber Poenitentialis*, one of the oldest existing codes of ecclesiastical law. Sacrifices to 'demons' earned a penance of between one and ten years. Killing a person by magic earned seven years penance, the first three involving fasting on bread and water. Raising storms by witchcraft earned five years penance, the first being spent on a bread and water fast.

These penalties became progressively harsher as time passed though never quite reached the level in England that they did in continental Europe because the Inquisition was not permitted to enter.

When the Inquisition was founded in 1230 it was to prevent the spread of heresy. It was not allowed to investigate witchcraft until the fourteenth century when it won the right by arguing that witchcraft was the greatest heresy of all because it involved submission to the Devil instead of God. Several Popes in the fourteenth and

ON THE MORNING of the Battle of Hastings, William of Normandy happened to put his body armour on back to front. This was a very bad omen but he is said to have declared: "If I believed in sorcery I would not go to battle today, but I have never put my trust in sorcery." He went ahead with the battle and of course defeated Harold to become William the Conqueror of England.

Four years later however, William was persuaded to try using witchcraft in his hunt for the Saxon rebel Hereward the Wake, who was hiding out with his followers in the fens of East Anglia. One of William's knights, Ivo Taillebois, recommended a particularly powerful witch who was put up in lodgings in Brandon near Thetford while the king gathered his troops. Unfortunately for him, Hereward happened to lodge at the same house while in the disguise of a travelling potter. He overheard the witch discussing her plan with their landlady and had time to set a trap of his own.

On the appointed day the witch was set on a tall wooden tower and began chanting her spells aimed at giving courage to the king's men and disheartening the rebels. The rebels, however, just set fire to the reed beds and, aided by a strong wind, soon engulfed the Normans in smoke and flame. They scattered in panic and many drowned in the fens or were picked off easily by rebel archers. It was a complete rout and William was lucky to escape with his life. The witch fell from her tower and broke her neck.

fifteenth centuries gave their explicit blessing to the Inquisition's methods of attacking witchcraft.

In 1486 two Inquisitors, Heinrich Kramer and Jakob Sprenger, wrote one of the most influential manuals of witch finding ever. The *Malleus Maleficarum* (or Hammer of the Witches) was endorsed by Pope Innocent VIII and became a standard handbook for judges across Europe for almost three centuries, running to fourteen editions between its publication and 1520.

Most of what we know about witches during the period of their great persecution comes from the records of their persecutors because they left virtually no written accounts themselves. Even though the testimony is often in the form of their own confessions at trial, we have to remember that these confessions were usually extracted by torture. They were telling their inquisitors what they wanted to hear, often with much prompting in the form of leading questions, to which even a nod or groan would count as admission.

Witches' confessions in court records tell us more about what people believed about witches at the time than what the individuals making them had actually been up to.

For about three centuries, between the end of the Middle Ages around 1450 and the Enlightenment in 1750 the persecution of witches in Europe was on a scale to match the periodic genocide of Jews, Gypsies and other scape-goats for the evils of the day. Over 100,000 witch trials are

on record across Europe, leading to execution in over half the cases. Overall about three quarters of condemned witches were female.

In France in the seventeenth century it is believed that up to 30,000 people were burned at the stake as convicted witches or werewolves.

Although the interrogators, judges and executioners of witches were exclusively male, their accusers were as likely to be female as male.

The traditional tolerance of wise women and 'cunning men' in the Middle Ages was shaken by the Black Death that swept Europe in 1347-9, carrying off one in three of the population. In England alone the plague killed 1.5 million out of an estimated population of 4 million.

In a climate where every natural disaster was believed to be designed by either God or the Devil, people searched

SHE CHURCH, which had always been hostile to wise women and men and all other remnants of pre-Christian faith (such as fertility festivals) but forced to tolerate much, took advantage of the situation.

There was considerable resistance to abandoning many of the old ways however, and it was not till the start of the seventeenth century that the authorities felt bold enough to lash out against all challenges, as epitomised in William Perkins' 1608 polemic *Discourse on the Damned Art of Witchcraft* which argued that good witches were even more dangerous than bad ones and they should all be killed:

> *. . . by witches we understand not only those which kill and torment: but all Diviners, Charmers, Jugglers, all Wizards commonly called wise men and women; yea whosoever do anything (knowing what they do) which cannot be effected by nature or art; and in the same number we reckon all good Witches, which do no hurt but good, which do not spoil and destroy, but save and deliver . . . Men do commonly spit at the damnifying Sorcerer, as unworthy to live among them; whereas the other is so dear unto them that they hold themselves and their country blessed that have him among them, they fly unto him in necessity, they depend upon him as their god, and by this means thousands are carried away into their final confusion. Death therefore is the just and deserved portion of the good Witch.*

their consciences and imaginations for causes rather than looking for natural explanations. In a very real sense the Church and general population believed during those hard times that they were under siege by Satan and his demons and agents, such as sorcerers and heretics.

Convinced that supernatural forces were at work, suspicion gradually focussed on witches, reaching a peak of hysteria between 1550 and 1650 when the majority of trials and executions took place. After that the numbers fell rapidly and ended almost completely by the mid eighteenth century.

Besides natural disasters, this was also a period of intellectual ferment with the Renaissance and the Reformation both unsettling people's view of the world and their place in it. Many historians blame witch hunts and other outbreaks of hysteria at the time on a reaction to chaos and uncertainty, as old certainties gave way to a fresh and materialistic world view.

In Elizabethan England the Witchcraft Act of 1563 was passed 'agaynst Conjuracions Inchauntmentes and Witchecraftes'. This gave new formalised powers to witch hunters. Harsh though the law was by modern standards, it was more lenient than in neighbouring countries and witchcraft was considered a civil crime (*maleficum*), not heresy.

Torture of suspects was not officially permitted under the English Witchcraft Act but even without it many accused witches seem to have freely confessed to wild supernatural practices, including mating with the Devil. Probably this is due to the prevailing definitions of torture at that time.

Of 270 Elizabethan witch trials on record, 247 were of women and just 23 of men. The women were usually old, poor and lived alone.

Many of the accused had formerly been considered 'wise women' because of their knowledge of herbal and other remedies. This was now held against them as the distinction between White and Black witches was blurred by hysteria.

Psycho-active plants such as mandrake, monkshood, cannabis, belladonna, henbane and hemlock were common ingredients in many folk remedies at the time, not just witches' brews.

In continental Europe the Catholic Church included knowledge of herbal medicine in its definition of witchcraft because: "those who used herbs for cures did so only through a pact with the Devil".

Hanging was the usual form of execution for witches in England rather than burning, as in France, Spain and other European countries. This was because witchcraft was considered a crime rather than heresy, for which the penalty *was* being burned alive.

MOTHER SHIPTON

A SHINING EXCEPTION to the general trend of witch persecution is the case of Mother Shipton, England's most famous prophetess. She was often accused of witchcraft throughout her life but managed to live to a healthy old age and, as far as is known, died peacefully in her bed at the age of 73 in 1561, a death which she had herself predicted.

Her story was not written down for almost a century and so it is likely that much of it (and her prophecies) has been embellished, but there is no doubting her fame in her own lifetime and the seriousness with which her prophecies were taken. After the Great Fire of London in 1666 Samuel Pepys commented: "See - Mother Shipton's word is out" for she had predicted that the houses of London would fall and men walk upon their rooftops, that the city would be ruined and scarcely a house left to provide a flagon of wine.

Mother Shipton was born Ursula Sontheil (or Southeil) on a July night in 1488, in a cave by the River Nidd in Knaresborough Forest, North Yorkshire. The cave is close to a mysterious spring considered magical at the time which has the curious property of petrifying anything left in its apparently clear waters. Both can be visited to this day.

Her mother Agatha was just fifteen at the time, a girl of loose morals bordering on prostitution. A woman helping at the birth claimed that when the baby was born there was a great stench of sulphur and

a mighty crack of thunder outside. This led to rumours that she had been fathered by the Devil, rumours helped by the precocious talent for prophecy that she displayed from an early age.

She was also said to be enormous at birth and deformed in some unspecified way. Not a very promising start to life, especially as she was given up for adoption at the age of two so her mother could enter a convent in Nottingham where she spent the rest of her days. Nevertheless Ursula prospered modestly and at the age of 24 married Toby Shipton, a carpenter. They had no children but seem to have been happy enough and meanwhile Ursula's reputation for uncanny predictions spread across Yorkshire and beyond, reaching as far as London and King Henry VIII's own ears.

Henry VIII was just beginning his turbulent reign when Mother Shipton married, and many of her most famous prophecies concerned his fortunes. Regarding his invasion of France (whose emblem was the lily) she is said to have prophesied:

> "*When the English Lion shall set his paw on the Gallic shore, then shall the Lilies begin to droop for fear; there shall be much weeping and wailing amongst the ladies of that country, because the Princely Eagle shall join with the Lion to tread down all that shall oppose them.*"

After an unpromising start to the invasion Henry finally triumphed over the French in 1513 at Guinegate (now Enguinegatte) with the aid of mercenaries supplied by the Emperor Maximilian of Austria (the 'Princely Eagle'). This became known as the Battle of the Spurs supposedly because of the haste with which the French troops fled.

Mother Shipton is also said to have incurred the wrath of Cardinal Wolsey, Henry VIII's right hand man, whom she dubbed the 'Mitred Peacock' because of his extravagance. Finally she predicted he would not visit York again, of which he was Archbishop. He set out for York in 1530 both to prove her wrong and burn her at the stake, but when in sight of the city he was recalled to London on a charge of treason and died of illness on the way.

Many people, incidentally, suspected Wolsey himself of having used sorcery to rise from his humble origins to the second most powerful position in the land. But few dared say so publicly before his death.

Mother Shipton by contrast lived to see the start of Elizabeth I's glorious reign and although it is impossible to know how many of her surviving prophecies were later forged to fit events, what is certain is that enough came true in her own lifetime to earn her an awesome reputation and this epitaph on her tomb:

> *Here lies she who never lied;*
> *Whose skill often has been tried:*
> *Her prophecies shall still survive,*
> *And ever keep her name alive.*

Sadly her most famous prophecies in which she seemed to predict the modern world in uncanny detail almost certainly were forged in 1862 by Charles Hindley, the editor of the collection of her prophecies that he published that year:

> *Carriages without horses shall go,*
> *And accidents fill the world with woe.*
> *Around the world thoughts shall fly*
> *In the twinkling of an eye.*
> *The world upside down shall be*
> *And gold be found at the root of a tree.*
> *Through hills man shall ride,*
> *And no horse be at his side.*
> *Under water men shall walk,*
> *Shall ride, shall sleep, shall talk.*
> *In the air men shall be seen,*
> *In white, in black, in green;*
> *Iron in the water shall float,*
> *As easily as a wooden boat.*

Queen Elizabeth I's mother, Anne Boleyn, was accused by her enemies of being a witch because she had a sixth finger on one hand and a prominent mole on her neck (witch's teat). Elizabeth herself had a keen interest in astrology, alchemy and other 'occult' practices which may have influenced the relative leniency of the English witchcraft laws.

The first notable witch trial in England under the 1563 Act took place in Chelmsford, Essex, in 1566. Elizabeth Frances, Agnes Waterhouse and her daughter Joan were accused of being witches by a range of witnesses, including a child, with wild and colourful accusations.

Under examination Agnes confessed to having kept a 'familiar' she called Satan, which would do whatever she asked for payment, usually, of a chicken and a drop of her own blood. Originally it was in the form of an old white spotted cat that she kept in a pot. Later it was usually a toad but it could take any form. In the shape of a black, horned dog it had terrorised a neighbour Agnes Brown, twelve years old at the time, for not freely sharing her butter. This familiar was supposed to be able to talk as clearly as any human.

Agnes Waterhouse was hanged, possibly being the first person hanged for witchcraft in England. Elizabeth Francis was jailed for a year, but twelve years later was convicted and hanged for another charge of witchcraft. Joan Waterhouse was cleared.

An eighth of the Assize trials in Essex during the 1580s were for witchcraft. Of the sixty-four accused, fifty-three were found guilty.

THE WITCHES OF WARBOYS

The Witches of Warboys are famous for having supposedly killed Oliver Cromwell's own grandmother.

It all began in November 1589 when Robert Throckmorton's ten-year-old daughter Jane began having fits and seizures during which she cried out that a certain Alice Samuel was tormenting her. Throckmorton was a resident of Warboys in the Cambridgeshire fens. Ignoring the girl's accusations at first, he called in the famous Dr Barrow of Cambridge, who reached the conclusion that the child was the victim of witchcraft.

Soon afterwards Jane's four sisters, an aunt and some servants went down with the same symptoms. All accused 76-year-old Alice Samuel of bewitching them but still the Throckmortons took no action against her and seem not to have believed the accusations.

Then a year or so later the Throckmortons received a sympathetic visit from Lady Cromwell, Oliver Cromwell's grandmother and wife of Sir Henry their

THE THREE JOANS

𝕬NOTHER FAMOUS TRIAL in Chelmsford in 1589 saw one man and nine women accused of witchcraft. Three of the women, Joan Cunny, Joan Upney and Joan Prentice were hanged within a couple of hours of being sentenced. Of those remaining, four more were hanged and three found not guilty

During the trial Joan Cunney of Stysted, about 80 years old at the time, confessed to having learned the art of witchcraft from a certain 'mother Humfrye of Maplested' and had been practising it for the past twenty years.

Using her new skills she had drawn a magic circle in a field, uttered a prayer to Satan that she had since forgotten, and summoned two demons in the shape of black toads. They could speak and named themselves Jack and Jill. Jack would harm men and Jill women. Later she acquired two more toad familiars, Nicholas and Ned. Nicholas specialised in killing horses and Ned went for cattle. The witch fed them on white bread and milk.

Cunney said she used her imps to avenge herself for any wrongs and slights from her neighbours. Sometimes it happened that their faith in God was too strong for them to be attacked directly, as with the local minister, in which case their family, servants and livestock had been made to suffer and even die.

While saying that she had hurt too many people

to remember exactly, Joan Cunney confessed to causing by witchcraft several known instances of misfortune, illness and death. Her young grandsons, ten or twelve years old, named several more cases and became the chief witnesses against her.

Joan Upney likewise confessed to having familiars in the shape of toads or moles that she sent against her enemies. Joan Prentice's familiar was a brown ferret called Bidd that used to come at bedtime when she called three times: "Bidd, come Bidd, come suck." Then he would run up and stand on her shoulder to suck blood from her cheek, after which he would do whatever mischief she asked.

landlord. When she heard their tale Lady Cromwell sent for Alice Samuel, who was also a tenant, roughly accused her of witchcraft and snipped off a lock of her hair for Mrs Throckmorton to burn and thus break the spell.

Alice Samuel was outraged and muttered some rash words that were later held against her. Lady Cromwell that night had a nightmare involving Alice Samuel and her cat and from that moment her health declined. She died fifteen months later in 1592.

Meanwhile Alice Samuel had been taken before the Bishop of Lincoln and two local justices of the peace, accused of bewitching the Throckmorton children, who had continued to languish. The children then accused her not only of bewitching them but of having killed Lady Cromwell with the aid of her husband Samuel and daughter Agnes. The three were taken to Huntingdon Assizes where on 5 April 1593 they were found guilty on all charges and hanged.

Their worldly goods were used to fund an annual sermon against witchcraft in Huntingdon by a Fellow of Queen's College, Cambridge. This continued until 1814, though by the end the tone had changed from warning against the dangers of witchcraft to warning against the superstition of believing in it.

In 1604 in the first year of his reign King James I introduced a new and much more severe Witchcraft Act to replace the Elizabethan one.

At Chelmsford, there was a mass trial in 1645 that launched the career of 'Witchfinder General' Matthew Hopkins in which thirty-two women were accused of witchcraft and twenty-nine hanged.

WITCH CURSES

Witches were believed capable of bringing
harm to others in any number of ways.

An evil look or simple curse was often believed
enough to cause death, especially if the curse had
been written down or engraved into metal or wood.

More likely to be effective though was the witch doll,
in which an effigy was made of the cursed person,
linked to them in a variety of ways. It could be a doll
made of corn, wax or wood into which the victim's
hair or clothing was worked. Or it could be a rough
carving of their face engraved with their name. The
effigy could then be thrown on the fire for a sudden
end or left to rot for a slow one. Or it could be
stabbed with pins, drowned or tortured in a variety of
ingenious ways.

A witch's imps could be sent in a variety of guises to
milk or blight a neighbour's cows and goats.

Any old garment of an enemy could be used to kill
them if buried secretly in an existing grave.

MATTHEW HOPKINS, WITCHFINDER GENERAL

Hath not this present Parliament
A Lieger to the Devil sent,
Fully impowered to treat about
Finding revolted Witches out?
And has he not within a year
Hanged threescore of them in one Shire?
Some only for not being drowned,
And some for sitting above ground
Whole days and nights upon their Breeches,
And feeling pain, were hanged for Witches.

From Samuel Butler's *Hudibras* 1663

Matthew Hopkins, the infamous Witchfinder General, was responsible for the deaths of more 'witches' than anyone else in England during his reign of terror in 1645-6. Together with his partner John Stearne he sent at least 230 to the gallows in fourteen months, and probably many more; and for each death he was paid handsomely in silver and gold.

Hopkins' early life is obscure but it seems likely that he was one of six children of James Hopkins, the vicar of Great Wenham in Suffolk from 1612 until he died in 1634. Matthew probably grew up and studied partly in the Netherlands where his family had connections and where he may have been inspired to become a 'witch-pricker'. He only firmly enters the record in 1641 when he bought some property near Manningtree, Essex, probably with his inheritance.

He also had a share in the Old Thorn Inn in Mistley, a village on the coast near Manningtree. The Thorn was later to become famous as his centre of operations, where he received informers and built a network of political connections including John Thurlowe, chief of Cromwell's Secret Service (this was during the Civil War and Essex was a Roundhead strong-hold), and William Lilly, one of the most famous astrologers of the day.

Hopkins' job initially was as clerk to a ship owner in Mistley and he seems to have been a minor lawyer. Certainly he made a close study of the laws relating to witchcraft, which he ably manipulated to his own advantage.

Using his contacts and armed with little more than King James I's *Daemonologie* (1597) and a couple of other books on witch hunting and the laws relating to it, Hopkins set himself up as a witch-finder in 1645, claiming a special commission from Parliament and offering to root out witches for often quite extravagant fees.

His anti-witch crusade began in Maningtree, leading to a notorious mass trial in Chelmsford after which twenty-nine women were hanged for witchcraft. Soon afterwards four more joined them for allegedly sending a bear to attack Hopkins.

His fame from the Chelmsford trial enabled Hopkins to spread his campaign into Suffolk where he again caused a sensation by proving that the unpopular

80-year-old minister of Brandeston, John Lowes, was a witch. The interrogation method was to have him "*kept awake several nights together while running him backwards and forwards about his cell until out of breath. After a brief rest, they then ran him again. And thus they did for several days and nights together, till he was weary of his life and scarce sensible of what he said or did*".

At which point he signed a confession that he had made a pact with the Devil and suckled four familiars called Tom, Flo, Bess and Mary. With these imps he had bewitched cattle and caused a ship to sink off Harwich with the loss of fourteen lives. Lowes later retracted this confession but was hanged anyway, having to say his own prayers on the way to the scaffold because no other minister would do it for him.

Soon Hopkins and Stearne were so busy they took on four helpers but their days in the limelight were numbered. Both the morality and legality of his proceedings were increasingly questioned till finally Parliament set up its own commission to look into the witchcraft problem and ordered him to desist in 1646.

Hopkins retired to Manningtree where he died a year later, probably of consumption though there is a more colourful legend recorded by William Andrews, a nineteenth century writer on Essex folklore. He said that Hopkins was accused of sorcery himself, of having used it to procure a list of all the witches in England; and that he had drowned during the 'swimming' test. That is probably wishful thinking. He is buried in Mistley where his ghost is said to haunt Mistley Pond, especially at Halloween.

As torture was not officially permitted under English law, Matthew Hopkins devised and adapted other methods of extracting confessions that skated just within it.

First there was the humiliation of subjects being publicly stripped and having their bodies intimately searched for incriminating extra nipples – moles or other marks that could be interpreted as 'devil's teats' for feeding their imps and familiars. Then beating, starvation and sleep deprivation often followed.

If this was not enough there was 'witch-pricking' wherein a variety of vicious spikes were used to probe the victim's body for the 'devil's spots', morbid areas of flesh that witches were supposed to have that did not bleed or feel pain. Hopkins is believed to have used spikes with retractable points for many such 'proofs'.

Stubborn subjects might also be tied in a restricted sitting position on a stool and left for a day or more till numb, then marched up and down, or made to run around the interrogation room without rest or sleep till they dropped.

Their floating on the water was appointed by God for a super-naturall signe of the monstrous impiete of the Witches, that the water shal refuse to receive them in her bosom, that have shaken off them the sacred Water of Baptisme, and willfullie refused the benefite thereof.

King James I *Daemonologie* 1597

'Swimming' or ducking a suspected witch had been popularised by King James I's tome *Daemonologie*. The principle was that as witches had rejected baptism at their initiation with Satan, so the element water would reject them. Hopkins devised his own version in which the suspects were bent double and had their thumbs bound to their toes. Then they were lowered into the water with a rope on each side, supposedly to stop them drowning if the water accepted them and they sank. Usually they were required to sink three times to prove their innocence and of course many accused witches simply drowned – innocent but dead.

'Swimming' witches was an elaboration of the old custom of ducking 'common scolds' who were defined as troublesome women who broke the public peace by habitually arguing and quarrelling with their neighbours. Under English law only women could be convicted of the offence and its Latin name *communis rixatrix* only has a female gender. Hot-tempered and quarrelsome men were also occasionally ducked though, as were brewers of bad beer and bakers of bad bread.

There stands, my friend, in yonder pool
An engine called the ducking-stool;
By legal power commanded down
The joy and terror of the town.
If jarring females kindle strife,
Give language foul, or lug the coif,
If noisy dames should once begin
To drive the house with horrid din,
Away, you cry, you'll grace the stool;
We'll teach you how your tongue to rule.

Benjamin West *The Ducking Stool* 1780

A preserved ducking-stool can still be seen in Canterbury and in many other places around Britain there are plaques recording where they stood.

The ducking-stool in Sandwich, Kent, bore the inscription: *Of members ye tonge is worst or beste. An yll tonge oft doth breede unreste.*

In actions of slander caused by a man s wife, after judg-
ment past for damages, the woman shall be punished by
Ducking, and if the slander be such as the damages shall
be adjudged as above 500 lbs. of Tobacco, then the woman
shall have a ducking for every 500 lbs. of Tobacco
adjudged against the husband if he refuse to pay the
Tobacco.

Statute Books of Virginia (1662)

In *The Percy Anecdotes*, a collection of curious observa-
tions by Reuben and Sholto Percy published in 1823, is a
tale that suggests the ducking stool was not always an
effective deterrent. They tell the story of a Mrs Finch who
was sentenced to ducking three times by the King's
Bench. On the fourth occasion she was fined three marks
instead and imprisoned until she could pay.

The use of water to test for witches dates back to ancient
Babylon where it is enshrined in the Laws of
Hammurabi.

Not everyone was caught up in the witch hunting hysteria,
but it took courage to speak out when it was at its
height because of the danger of being accused of supporting
witchcraft. The safe line was to accept the reality of witchcraft but question the credibility of most cases that came
to court. King James himself came to hold this view.
He didn't doubt his own *Daemonologie* but increasingly
questioned whether many accused witches were guilty of
anything more than unpopularity. After personally

exposing several miscarriages of justice, usually from false accusations motivated by greed or revenge, he demanded that his judges be more thorough in their investigations and punished some that had been careless.

The last recorded official execution for witchcraft in England was in March 1684 when Alice Molland was hanged in Exeter. Many more unofficial executions did happen later without the blessing of the law however, by mobs and individuals convinced they were ridding the world of evil.

In Scotland where James I of England had been King James VI, his handbook on demonology fired witch hunters with special zeal. His interest in the subject was inspired by one of the most famous Scottish witch trials at North Berwick in 1595 which he attended, personally taking charge of some interrogations, which were extracted under torture. The main charge against the accused was that through witchcraft they had raised a storm and fog to sink or turn back the king's ship as he was returning from Denmark with his new bride, Anne of Denmark in 1590. There had indeed been a great storm and a ship carrying the royal jewellery and wedding gifts did sink, but the king himself survived.

Anne's attempt to reach Scotland the previous year had also been foiled by storms that her Danish admirals had blamed on witchcraft, putting several suspects on trial. This most likely suggested the idea to James.

Agnes Sampson, a midwife from the Lothians, was
accused with several accomplices of having organised a
mass gathering of up to 200 other witches to work her
mischief. Riding 'seives and riddles' they had supposedly
gone to sea to raise a tempest in order to drown the king
and his bride. Also they were accused of having 'made
wax images and brewed poisons' to undermine his health.

Agnes Sampson confessed to having made a wax effigy of
the king which had been cursed by herself, nine other
witches and the Devil, who had attended their gathering
in person. To raise a storm against the king's ship they had
christened a cat, bound it to choice body parts of a dead
man and then thrown it into the sea to drown.

After coming ashore at North Berwick the witches were
also supposed to have had a wild dance to the music of
one Gillie Duncan, a servant girl of the Deputy-Bailiff of
Trenent. She was summoned to give a performance for
the king who found it enchanting, but nevertheless she
was tortured into confessing herself a witch and naming
many 'accomplices'. Agnes Sampson and about seventy
others were executed on Castle Hill in Edinburgh.

James suspected Francis, Earl of Bothwell, of having
commissioned the witches to kill him so he could become
king, but could not prove it and had to settle for driving
Bothwell into exile.

Witchcraft was a criminal offence in Scotland, from 1563
when it was included in a statute law by Mary Queen of

ONE OF THE MOST famous cases to emerge from the seventy convictions in the North Berwick trials was that of Dr John Fian (or Cunningham), a young schoolmaster from Saltpans whose story featured in a popular broadsheet about the trials called *Newes from Scotland*.

King James personally supervised his interrogation and passed sentence. Among the tortures employed were having his head bound with rope and then jerked violently in every direction. Then crushing boots were applied to his legs until he lost consciousness. This was considered a trick of the Devil to keep him from confessing so his tongue was then pricked with pins until he started talking. Then he escaped and went home to Saltpans, recanting his confession. But he was caught and tortured again by having his fingernails drawn and needles inserted.

Whatever he confessed under torture, Fian denied later when he was able but no notice was taken.

Among Fian's twenty-two charges was that of conspiring (along with Agnes Sampson) to wreck King James's ship by throwing a dead cat into the sea; making a covenant with Satan and receiving his mark; worshipping Satan in North Berwick church; having "ecstasies and trances" often for several hours while his spirit travelled; looting corpses for body parts to be used in witchcraft; opening locked doors by breathing on them; seducing thirty-two wives and widows; flying through the air; storm-raising and casting horoscopes.

Another charge was that he had attempted to use sorcery to cause a girl to fall in love with him. To this end he bribed her young brother, who shared her bed, to "obtaine for him three hairs of his sisters privities". She woke while he attempted this and complained to her mother, who suspected what was going on. She gave her son three hairs pulled from a heifer's udder which he passed on to John Fian. Fian cast his spell and was immediately followed everywhere by a love-sick heifer. It even followed him into church one day, which was when people first began to suspect him of having dealings with the Devil.

Fian was also accused of riding with a companion who had "by his devilish craft" conjured magical torches for their horse which had lit the night up as bright as day, and had used the torches to kill an enemy as he entered his house.

The gallows in the woodcut illustrate John Fian's end though he was not actually hanged. Like most of his fellow Scottish 'witches' he was strangled at the stake and burned to ashes.

Newes from Scotland.

Scots, until its repeal in 1736. The danger of witchcraft was one of the few matters on which the Protestant and Catholic Churches of Scotland were in complete agreement.

In the century from 1563 an estimated 4,500 mostly female witches were executed, four times as many as in England which had five times the population. Only in Germany were witches persecuted more fiercely.

Forms of torture commonly employed on Scottish witch suspects included: keeping the prisoner awake for several days and nights; tying her naked to a cold stone for up to a month; solitary confinement in a dark, cramped cell; flogging; crushing hands, feet and legs; pulling out finger-nails; soaking a hair shirt in vinegar so the skin could be pulled off the body.

In June 1596 Alison Margaret Balfour was kept with her arms in a vice for two days while forced to watch her family being tortured. Her 81-year-old husband was crushed by 700 pounds of iron bars. Her son had his feet crushed to pulp in the Spanish Boots while her seven-year-old daughter was given the thumbscrews or 'pilli-winks'. Her servant Thomas was clamped in the vice for ten days and scourged till "there was neither flesh nor hide upon him". Both recanted their confessions on release from torture but were executed anyway.

A single accusation of witchcraft to the Church in Scotland was enough to trigger an investigation.

THE LAST WITCH OF SCOTLAND

THE LAST PERSON to be convicted in Britain under the 1736 Witchcraft Act was Helen Duncan in 1944 because of fears that she might clairvoyantly betray details of the D-Day landings to the Germans. She was jailed for nine months. This was the first time the Act had been used for over a century and the case led to it being finally repealed in 1951.

Helen Duncan is often known as the Last Scottish Witch because of her conviction. She had been born in Callander, Stirlingshire, in 1897 and became a medium, travelling throughout Britain. Her speciality was producing ectoplasm, the cloud-like substance beloved of Victorian mediums, which appeared to give substance to the departed so that they could actually touch their grieving relatives and friends.

In 1941 Helen Duncan caused a stir at one of her séances by announcing the sinking of the HMS Barham in the Mediterranean after apparently contacting the spirit of one of its dead sailors. This was perfectly true; the ship had been sunk by the German U-Boat U331 with the loss of 861 lives but the War Office had suppressed news of the incident and did not confirm it till several months later. Her arrest and conviction at the Old Bailey under the antiquated law appeared to be designed to prevent a repeat of the incident, since secrecy was almost essential to the success of the Normandy landings.

A bronze bust of Helen Duncan presented to the town of Callander stirred such controversy that it is now only to be seen at the Smith Art Gallery and Museum in Stirling.

Anyone who consulted witches in Scotland was considered as guilty as the witches themselves.

Janet Wishart was tried and condemned for witchcraft in Aberdeen in 1596; being accused, among many other things of having caused many of her neighbours to waste away and die. In her 'confession' she admitted to having attended, with her son Thomas Lees, the great gathering of witches at the Market and Fish Crosses at midnight on Halloween 1595 where the devil had entertained them with diabolical musical instruments. Many at the gathering had been in the form of cats and hares, Scottish witches' favourite guises. Her son was also executed but other members of the family were cleared and only banished.

Between February 1596 and April 1597 twenty-three women and one man were tried and convicted for witchcraft in Aberdeen.

Those found guilty of witchcraft in Scotland were usually strangled at a stake and then coated with pitch and set alight. Only a minority considered the worst cases were burned alive.

The last known witch-burning in Scotland took place in Dornach, Invernesshire, in 1722. There were strong protests from some churches when the witchcraft laws were reformed in 1736.

The 1736 Witchcraft Act of King George II revoked the penalty of hanging for witchcraft throughout Britain. It was reduced to a misdemeanour equivalent to fraudu-lence. The offence was pretending to be a witch, not witchcraft itself, and was punishable only by fines and imprisonment.

THE PITTENWEEM WITCHES

In 1704 in the Fife fishing village of Pittenweem, Mrs Beatrix Laing made the mistake of getting into an argu-ment with Patrick Morton, the blacksmith's son. She wanted him to make her some nails but he told her she would have to wait. She went off muttering against him. The next day he saw her throwing hot ashes into a tub of water, which he had heard was part of casting spells.

Soon afterwards Patrick lost his appetite and began to shed weight. Then he began having fits, during which he accused Beatrix Laing and others of having enchanted him. He also claimed the Devil had appeared and tried to make him renounce Jesus.

At the urging of the local minister, the town elders obtained an arrest warrant from the Privy Council and Beatrix Laing was jailed and tortured into confessing witchcraft and implicating neighbours. She retracted the confession as soon as she could and some moderate elders obtained her release with a fine. She was shunned by everybody though and had to move to St Andrews.

Thomas Brown, another of the accused, died of star-vation in Pittenweem gaol. A third, Janet Corphat, was lynched. Urged on by the minister a mob broke into the prison and dragged her off to the beach where she was beaten and then crushed to death beneath a door and boulders. Still unsatisfied, they then drove a horse-drawn sledge backwards and forwards over her corpse, which was later buried in the communal grave at Witch's Corner.

$\mathcal{I}$T HAS TO BE remembered that the torture of suspects for all kinds of crimes was common practice all over Europe at the time of the witch trials. Here is a tariff approved for torturers by the Archbishopric of Cologne in 1757:

Pricelist (Reichsthaler / Albus)

1. For tearing apart and quartering by four horses 5/26
2. For quartering 4/0
3. For the necessary rope for that purpose 1/0
4. For hanging the four quarters in four corners, the necessary rope, nails, chains, and the transport included 5/26
5. For beheading and burning, everything included 5/26
6. For the necessary rope for this proceedure, and for preparing and igniting the stake 2/0
7. For strangling and burning 4/0
8. For rope and for preparing and igniting the stake 2/0
9. For burning alive 4/0
10. For rope and for preparing and igniting the stake 2/0
11. For breaking alive on the wheel 4/0
12. For rope and chains for this proceedure 2/0 Etc.

DIARY OF A DAY'S TORTURE

EYEWITNESS REPORT of the first day of an accused witch's torture at Prossneck in Germany in 1629 and recounted in Wilhelm Pressel's study *Hexen und Hexenmeister* (1860):

She was bound to the rack and her hair cut short. Alcohol was rubbed into the remaining hair which was then set alight and burned to the roots. This was to reveal any witch marks it might conceal.

Strips of sulphur were fixed under her arms and set alight.

Her hands were tied behind her back and she was hoisted by them into the air, where she was left hanging while her torturer went to breakfast.

When he returned he threw alcohol over her back and lit it.

Heavy weights were attached to her body and she was

In 1562 an unseasonable hailstorm hit Wiesensteig in Germany, destroying the entire crop. Witchcraft was suspected and in the ensuing trials 62 suspects were found guilty and executed.

Witches have always been believed to have control over the weather. Usually that meant they were blamed for any sudden bad weather but sailors long used to resort to wise women and cunning men to buy favourable winds for their next voyage.

A visitor to the Isle of Man in the fourteenth century commented on the women selling winds in the ports.

hoisted again for a while before being lowered and squeezed against a spiked plank. Over the next few hours her thumbs, big toes, calves and legs were all squeezed in a vice and she was whipped till blood flowed, all these torments alternating with questions.

Then the torturer and court officials took a couple of hours for lunch, leaving her thumbs and big toes in the vice.

That afternoon an official came who disapproved of the harsh questioning, but the suspect was severely whipped again anyway before being left to recover. The next day it all started again . . .

They came in the form of a cord with three knots. When the first was loosed a mild wind would spring up. The second released a strong wind and the third a gale. This practice continued in some places right into the nineteenth century.

In 1814 Sir Walter Scott purchased a wind in Stromness from Bessie Miller.

In south-west France a group of witches was accused of having flown across the Atlantic on broomsticks to join their husbands who were fishing off Newfoundland.

═══ THE SALEM WITCH TRIALS ═══

The Salem witch trials of 1692 are one of the most closely documented and analysed outbreaks of witch hunting mania on record.

Part of the background that contributed to the hysteria was a climate of hostility between Salem Town and Salem Village, an attached agricultural and largely Puritan district that wanted to break away and form its own community. The first step towards this had been employing its own church minister.

Other factors were political uncertainty, fear of attack by Indians, fear of epidemics and a readiness to believe that supernatural forces were influencing all these things – they were either God's punishment or the Devil's doing.

The accidental trigger of the outbreak was the minister of Salem Village, Samuel Parris, and the female slave Tituba he had brought with him from Barbados.

Parris was married with a daughter Betty and orphaned niece Abigail. Unknown to the minister, the girls began to entertain themselves by forming a magic circle with several friends and dabbling in fortune telling and other minor magic. One of their favourite practices was reading the future by means of egg-white suspended in water. In their magic games they were coached by the slave Tituba, who also fed them lurid tales of witchcraft back in the Caribbean.

Finally Betty, the daughter, and Abigail grew afraid of what they were doing and began acting strangely enough for Samuel Parris to notice. Betty also suffered from a strange wasting disease. Her father called in a doctor who could find no physical cause, so they suspected witchcraft. Samuel interrogated Betty and suspicion quickly fell on Tituba.

Betty's friends also named two other women, Sarah

Osborne and Sarah Good. Sarah Osborne was an unpopular old lady who had given up attending religious meetings and Sarah Good was a beggar who was already suspected of bewitching the livestock of people who refused her alms.

Two magistrates, members of the Massachussets Bay Colony legislature, were sent to conduct the investigation. They were John Hathorne and Jonathan Corwin. Neither had any formal training in either the law or witch hunting, but they prepared themselves with books such as the *Malleus Maleficarum*, or *Hammer of the Witches* (1486), *A Discourse on the Damned Art of Witchcraft* (1608) and *Late Memorable Provinces* (1689) by Cotton Mather, a Boston minister who had dealt with an outbreak of witchcraft in his own parish.

John Hathorne was the great-great-grandfather of the writer Nathaniel Hawthorne, who added a 'w' to his name to distance himself from his witch-hunting ancestor.

No torture was sanctioned by the law in New England for witch investigations, but under interrogation in the Salem Village Meetinghouse the slave Tituba immediately and apparently freely confessed for three days, telling a wild story in which she had made a devilish compact with a tall man dressed in black who had made her sign a book in which she had read the names of the Sarahs Osborne and Good, plus others which she could not read.

The slave's motives for her confession are obscure. It's possible that she hoped to escape punishment by telling the magistrates all they wanted to hear. And this may even have worked because there seems to be a record of Tituba being sold by Parris after the fuss was all over to pay for her jail costs.

Betty, Abigail and six other girls were present at the

interrogations and were frequently seized with wild paroxysms.

Sarah Osborne and Sarah Good denied the accusations but were jailed anyway on the strength of Tituba's confession. Sarah Osborne died in prison two months later of natural causes.

The girls then began accusing others and by May 1692 over 200 people were imprisoned in Boston on suspicion of witchcraft. To cope with the crisis Governor Phips established a new Court of Oyer and Terminer to try the cases. The girls were present at the hearings.

In the Salem witch trials the first sign the inquiring magistrates, John Hathorne and Jonathan Corwin, looked for was a 'witch's nipple', a mole or other birthmark that might be used to suckle demons.

Circumstantial evidence was taken seriously, such as that after an argument one party's cow dropped mysteriously dead.

An inability to recite the Lord's Prayer without error was a strong mark of guilt.

The first case was that of Bridget Bishop. She had been accused and cleared of witchcraft twelve years before, but since then witch dolls had been found in the walls of her cellar during repairs, and on this evidence she was found guilty and hanged on Gallows Hill on 10 June.

Four more convictions soon followed and when a fifth suspect, Rebecca Nurse, was acquitted, the girls threw such a fit that the jury reversed its verdict and Rebecca Nurse was hanged with the others on 19 June.

These executions only served to inflame the hysteria in New England and both accusations and apparent victims of witchcraft multiplied. More convictions and executions followed, many of them on the strength of the girls' testimony that the accused had appeared to them in 'spectral' form to torment them.

Three of the convictions in particular sowed doubts about the girls' testimony.

Before his execution the Rev George Burroughs (the former Salem Village minister accused by the girls of being the instigator of all witchcraft in the area) recited the Lord's Prayer perfectly, something which witches were supposedly unable to do.

Giles Corey refused to dignify the charges against him with a reply. The court ordered him to be taken to a field near the Salem Meetinghouse and have rocks piled on his chest until his tongue was loosened. He died under the weight two days later.

Mary Easty, a sister of Rebecca Nurse, wrote to the court before her own hanging: "I know I must die, and my appointed time is set. But the Lord He knows it is, if it be possible, that no more innocent blood be shed, which undoubtedly cannot be avoided in the way and course you go in. I question not but your honors do to the utmost of your powers in the discovery and detecting of witchcraft and witches, and would not be guilty of innocent blood for the world. But by my own innocency I know you are in the wrong way. The Lord in his infinite mercy direct you in this great work, if it be His blessed will, that innocent blood be not shed."

In October 1692 Governor Phips gave orders protecting the accused from harm. He also suspended all but the most necessary arrests of new suspects and dissolved the Court of Oyer and Terminer. The last witch trial was in January 1693 and in May the Governor pardoned the remaining accused. Thus the Salem witch trials came to an end after nineteen hangings and one death by crushing.

There were no more witch trials in the US after Salem.

Salem Village finally separated from Salem Town in 1752, renaming itself Danvers.

In 1953 Henry Miller (1915 – 2005) dramatised the Salem affair in his play *The Crucible* as an allegory for the McCarthyite communist hysteria in the US at the time. In 1956 he was called before the House Committee on Un-American Activities and the following year was convicted of contempt of Congress for not revealing the identities of a literary circle believed to have communist links. This was quashed in 1958 by the Court of Appeals.

In 1957 *The Crucible* was first adapted for the cinema by Jean Paul Satre. In 1996 Miller was nominated for an Academy Award for his own screenplay for the movie directed by Nicholas Hytner and starring Daniel Day-Lewis, Winona Ryder and Paul Schofield.

Chapter IV

Witchcraft Today

In Europe and North America witch-hunting in the literal sense more or less died with the eighteenth century but other parts of the world are less fortunate. Sub-Saharan Africa in particular currently seems to be experiencing a surge almost equal to the worst that went on in sixteenth and seventeenth century Europe. Thousands of suspected witches are dying each year at the hands of mobs and vigilantes.

As before, the majority of victims are elderly women living on their own, often suspected of witchcraft simply because they have reached a respectable age while others have not. But significant numbers of men are also killed, usually traditional healers suspected of having turned to black magic.

On 22 August 1999 the London *Sunday Telegraph* reported the Tanzanian Ministry of Home Affairs claim that up to 5,000 people were lynched for suspected witchcraft between 1994 and 1998. Police records were more optimistic but still showed almost 400 such deaths

in an eighteen month period. Most of the victims were beaten or burned to death by gangs of youths. Some of the victims were accused simply on the grounds of having red eyes, a common consequence of years spent cooking in a smoky hut.

In Zimbabwe the persecution has mirrored the country's decline into economic chaos. Gordon Chavanduka, head of the Zimbabwe National Traditional Healers Association, said in 1999: "It's obvious the cause is economic. The worse the economy gets, the more political tension there is in society, the more frustrated and frightened people get. They turn to witchcraft to gain riches or to hurt their enemies."

The hysteria is fuelled by widespread trade in human body parts across Africa for use in magic, such parts often being obtained by ritual human sacrifice. This was suspected in the case of the torso of a five- or six-year-old African boy washed up near Tower Bridge in London in September 2001. The investigation centred on Nigeria but reached as far as South Africa with a special appeal by Nelson Mandela. It remains unsolved.

Credo Mutwa, internationally respected author on African traditions and himself a shamanic healer or *sangoma*, almost died when set upon by a witch-hunting mob in 1998. After being stabbed several times he lay helpless as they poured petrol to set him alight, but then he was saved by the very superstition that caused the attack. In his own words: "A young man shouted, 'His ghost will haunt you.' They vanished, leaving me like a fish on dry land."

South Africa's Northern Province is suffering particularly from witch-hunting hysteria thanks to poverty, insecurity and a lively tradition of magical belief that make a dangerous cocktail. Any sudden misfortune there is liable to be blamed on black magic and ten villages have had to be established as safe havens for people accused of witchcraft that dare not return to their homes.

Typical of the residents is 62-year-old Esther Rasesemola, who was accused of being a witch in 1990 after lightning struck her village. In her own words: "A group of people visited the *Inkanga* [traditional healer] to see who was responsible. When they returned, it was my brother-in-law who told the rest of the village that I was responsible. He owed me money and I think he did it to get rid of me because he did not want to pay the money back. People in the village became convinced I was a witch. They came to my house at night and burnt it down and took all my belongings. Then they put me in a truck and drove me to a deserted place and dropped me off with my husband and my three children. They told me never to come back to the village or they would kill me. My husband died two years after we were expelled. My children have gone away and now I have nothing. I don't believe in witchcraft. It is just superstitious belief."

Meanwhile in Kenya in 1993 'witches' were being killed at the rate of one a week in the Gusii tribe. A 99-year-old tribal elder Sanslaus Anunda revealed that in his youth the Gusii had an infallible method of detecting witches. When one was suspected the elders would gather and a certain mixture of herbs would be prepared. This was smeared on the hands of the suspect and a known innocent. Both then had to dip their hands in boiling water, then leave and return in five days. If the suspect's hands still showed any signs of burns she or he would be killed as a witch, but the innocent one's hands would always be perfectly healed.

GOOD WITCHES
OF THE WEST

While in Africa witch-hunting thrives in its old blood-thirsty way, in Europe, America and related cultures loosely called 'the West' witchcraft has shown a remark-able revival over the past century or two.

With the ending of the witch trials in Europe persecution continued for a while informally with beatings and lynchings unsanctioned by law, but these became increas-ingly rare. Wise women and men became quite a respected part of rural life again. In Britain the nineteenth century passion for collecting folklore led to many of these surviving witches being immortalised by vicars and other dignitaries intent on capturing the traditions of their parish or county.

Thanks to the Wise Man of Stokesley and others like him some of the ancient traditions of wise men and women survived long enough to be written about with sympa-thetic interest and provide fuel for the revival of interest in aspects of witchcraft today

Modern witchcraft does attract hostility, particularly from fundamentalist Christian groups who still see it as

THE WISE MAN
OF STOKESLEY

A FAMOUS 'CUNNING MAN' of the early nineteenth century was John Wrightson, known across North Yorkshire and Durham as the Wise Man of Stokesley. He attributed his talents to being the seventh son of a seventh daughter and claimed that normally he was no wiser than the next man but Knowledge came to him when he fasted. His special talents were curing animals, finding lost or stolen goods and seeing what was happening at a distance.

In *Forty Years in a Moorland Parish* by Rev JC Atkinson (1891) we hear how when recovering stolen goods Wrightson would always exact a promise from the owner not to take any further action if the goods were returned. Then he would cast a spell and usually within a few days the property would mysteriously reappear at the owner's house. The author suspected that fear of the Wise Man's powers alone was enough to make a thief repent.

Wrightson did not rely on the fears of the credulous alone, however. The story goes that one day two young stalwarts on their way to the Hiring Fair at Stokesley stopped off at his cottage "to have a bit of sport with old Wrightson".

The old man hospitably invited them in and built up the fire to take off their chill. They welcomed this at first but soon grew a bit too hot and then hotter still. The fire was blazing like a furnace and there they were hunched right over it and when they tried to move away they found they could not. Some strange power bound them where they were, unable to move a muscle.

The old man meanwhile chatted on amicably as if nothing was amiss till finally when they could bear no more, he broke the spell and turned them out into the night with a warning to think twice before trying to make a fool of him again.

the work of the Devil, but there is yet no sign of outright violent persecution. In broad swathes of society witchcraft or Wicca is accepted as just another expression of spirituality or religion and in North America many groups are officially registered as churches (such as the Covenant of Gaia Church in Alberta, Canada).

In 1965 the District Court of Virginia ruled that Wicca is a legally recognised religion entitled to all the benefits enjoyed by other accepted religions. This followed from the case of Dettmer v Landon.

Revived druids are permitted to welcome the midsummer sun at Stonehenge and the shelves of secular bookshops groan with witchcraft related volumes. In fiction Harry Potter has taken the world by storm while New Age shops are full of books of spells, incantations and generally helpful guidelines for budding witches.

Although some contemporary witches form organised covens with a religious hierarchy and formal ritual, many more practise individually or in small informal groups. These often call themselves Hedge Witches or Green Witches.

Among the organised Wiccan groups are to be found the Alexandrian, Blue Star, Celtic, Christian, Correllian, Dianic, Eclectic, Faery, Gardnerian (named after Gerald Gardner who is widely acclaimed the founder of modern witchcraft in the 1950s), Kemetic, Odyssean, Shakti, Stregheria and Universal Eclectic Wiccans.

Most modern Wiccans distance themselves completely from Satanism and Black Magic. Their aim is to recover the pagan traditions and beliefs (especially what is called Women's Wisdom) that were banned and demonised by Christianity.

FURTHER READING

The Complete Book of Spells & Curses
Leonard RN Ashley. Souvenir Press, New York 1999

The Hedge Witch's Way
Beth Rae. Robert Hale, London 2001

History of Witchcraft and Demonology
Montague Summers. Kessinger Publishing 2003

The Malleus Maleficarum
Jakob Sprenger, Heinrich Kramer
Trans. Montague Summers. Dover Publications 1971
www.malleusmaleficarum.org

The Virago Book of Witches
Ed. Shabrukh Husain. Virago Press, London 1993

Witchcraft and Black Magic
Summers, Montague. Dover Publications 2000

Witchcraft in Britain
Christina Hole. Paladin Books, London 1980

Witches
Hans Holzer. Black Dog & Leventhal 2002

ONLINE SOURCES

www.elizabethan-era.org.uk/elizabethan-witchcraft-and-witches.htm
www.gendercide.org/case_witchhunts.html
www.hulford.co.uk/intro.html
www.sacred-texts.com/pag/wcwe/
www.salemwitchtrials.com/salemwitchcraft.html
www.leopardmag.co.uk/feats/30/the-pursuit-of-witches/